Preface

This report examines the findings of Task 2 of the RAND study, "Analytic Architecture for Joint Staff Decision Support Activities." The project is sponsored by the Force Structure, Resources, and Assessment Directorate (J-8) within the Joint Staff. It documents our examination of the Joint Staff's analytic support requirements and its analytic framework, and recommends an analytic architecture structure.

The project consists of two tasks. In Task 1 of this study of analytic architecture, we sought to identify a number of existing or in-development architectures that could provide a viable structure and a common tableau. The strategy-to-tasks (STT) framework was identified, but it was undergoing modifications so it could be more jointly defined than in its original version. In Task 2 we developed STT further, as part of a more general analytic architecture, addressing questions regarding what an ideal analytic support architecture would look like and ways that this ideal architecture could be adopted by the Joint Staff.

This work was performed within the International Security and Defense Policy Center of RAND's National Defense Research Institute (NDRI), a federally funded research and development center sponsored by the Office of the Secretary of Defense, the Joint Staff, and the defense agencies. It should be of interest to those involved in the Planning, Programming, and Budgeting System (PPBS) process. Comments should be directed to the authors or to Dr. Gregory Treverton, Director of the International Security and Defense Policy Center.

Contents

Figures

Tables

Summary

This report examines what an ideal analytic support architecture would look like for the Joint Staff and the Chairman, Joint Chiefs of Staff (CJCS). It also looks at methods for incorporating the ideal framework into existing processes.

We designed the study as two tasks, together addressing five questions:

Task 1

1. What roles do the CJCS and Joint Staff play in Department of Defense (DoD) decisionmaking processes, particularly those involving resource identification and allocation?

2. Where do the various Planning, Programming, and Budgeting System (PPBS)-related processes involving the Joint Staff intersect?

3. What is the state of the Joint Staff's current analytic environment, and what information does it require to support well-informed decisionmaking?

Task 2

4. What would an ideal analytic support architecture look like?

5. How easily can existing processes accommodate recommended changes?

The research was motivated by the concern that in an increasingly complex analytic environment, the Joint Staff and the CJCS need an effective support framework to conduct analysis. Task 1 found that the Joint Staff's analytic environment has become fast-paced, demanding, and complex. It anticipated that increasing analytic support demands would be placed on the Joint Staff. Since the Task 1 report was written (see MR-511-JS), the Joint Staff has been designated as a major source of analysis for DoD, and it has become involved in the Joint Warfighting Capability Assessments (JWCAs). This report evaluates the use of the strategy-to-tasks (STT) framework, which was recommended in Task 1, and suggests organizational changes to enable a smooth transition to this analytic support architecture.

Our recommended "ideal" architecture is an expanded STT framework for representing the defense posture analytically, relating means to ends at four levels: policy, operations, assignment, and programming. This analytic representation would be informed by analysis of issues and by records of decisions made by the Secretary of Defense, the President, Congress, and others. The analytic representation would be an input to organizing and managing analysis. Similarly, Strategy-to-Tasks Resource Management (STRM) can be applied as a database to aid the Joint Staff in analysis. In addition, an "analytic toolbox" is suggested to aid the Joint Staff in undertaking analysis. These analytic tools include databases, political-military gaming, models, spreadsheets, and lessons learned.

Among the changes for the Joint Staff to consider are the following:

- Centralize technology, requirements, and acquisition functions.
- Consolidate modeling and simulation activities, which would be the underpinnings of the toolbox concept.
- Merge the exercise program responsibilities into operations.
- Strengthen links between the fiscally constrained strategy functions with force structure and resource assessments.
- Refine logistics requirements to reflect cross-service and Commander in Chief (CINC) requirements.

After describing the STT architecture, this report evaluates the analytic support architecture and how to implement change into the current structure. To identify key issues for analysis using the STT framework, we conducted a two-move research game that evaluated possible benefits of the proposed analytic architecture to raise and address key issues. An exercise on overseas presence, conducted for the J-5, enabled researchers to recognize that issues identified by game players could be organized, represented, and analyzed using the STT architecture. After rating the current analytic structure against the ideal one with respect to logic, ethics, and fairness, it was determined that the STT framework should be worked into the current structure.

The STT framework is helpful in understanding separate processes and relationships. It helps identify important issues and requirements and improves organizational efficiency and effectiveness.

Acknowledgments

The authors would like to thank Dr. Vincent P. Roske, who helped guide this project, and other members of the Joint Staff, who participated in discussions and workshops.

We would also like to thank RAND colleagues Bruce Bennett, Roger Brown, Paul Davis, Stephanie Deter, William Fedorochko, Mia Fromm, Michael Hix, Preston Niblack, C. Robert Roll, Bernard Rostker, Kathi Webb, and James Winnefeld for their insights and support.

Glossary

AOR	Area of Responsibility
ATACMS	Army Tactical Missile System
ATBM	Antitactical Ballistic Missile
BMD	Ballistic Missile Defense
BUR	Bottom-Up Review
BW	Biological Warfare
C4I	Command, Control, Communications, Computer Systems and Intelligence
CAT	Crisis Action Team
CINC	Commander in Chief
CJCS	Chairman of the Joint Chiefs of Staff
CONUS	Continental United States
CPA	Chairman's Program Assessment
CSPAR	CINC's Preparedness Assessment Report
CV	Aircraft Carrier
CVBG	Aircraft Carrier Battle Group
CVN	Nuclear Powered Aircraft Carrier
CW	Chemical Warfare
DoD	Department of Defense
DPG	Defense Planning Guidance
DPRK	Democratic People's Republic of Korea (North Korea)
FWE	Fighter-Wing Equivalent
GCC	Gulf Cooperation Council
IPL	Integrated Priority List
ISR	Intelligence, Surveillance, and Reconnaissance
JOT	Joint Operational Task
JPD	Joint Planning Document
JROC	Joint Requirements Oversight Council
JSCP	Joint Strategic Capabilities Plan
JSPS	Joint Strategic Planning System
JTASC	Joint Training and Simulation Center
JTF	Joint Task Force
JWCA	Joint Warfighting Capabilities Assessment
LOC	Line of Communication
LSA	Logistics Sustainability Analysis
MCM	Mine Countermeasures
MEU	Marine Expeditionary Unit
MNS	Mission Need Statement
MRC	Major Regional Conflict

NATO	North Atlantic Treaty Organization
NEO	Noncombatant Evacuation Operations
NIE	National Intelligence Estimate
NMS	National Military Strategy
NSS	National Security Strategy
ODS	Operation Desert Storm
OPTEMPO	Tempo of Operations
OSD	Office of the Secretary of Defense
PAR	Preparedness Assessment Report
PBD	Program Budget Decision
PERSTEMPO	Personnel Tempo
PES	Preparedness Evaluation System
PFP	Partnership For Peace
pol-mil	Political-Military
POM	Program Objective Memorandum
PPBS	Planning, Programming, and Budgeting System
prepo	Prepositioning
psyops	Psychological Operations
QA	Quality Assurance
QC	Quality Control
R&D	Research and Development
RC	Reserve Component
ROK	Republic of Korea
SecDef	Secretary of Defense
SLCM	Sea-launched cruise missile
SLOC	Sea Lines of Communication
SOF	Special Operations Force
STRM	Strategy-to-Tasks Resource Management
STT	Strategy-to-Tasks
TACWAR	Combat Assessment Model
TMD	Theater Missile Defense
USACOM	U.S. Atlantic Command
USAF	U.S. Air Force
USC	U.S. Code
USCENTCOM	U.S. Central Command
USEUCOM	U.S. European Command
USFK	U.S. Forces in Korea
USPACOM	U.S. Pacific Command
USSOCOM	U.S. Special Operations Command
USSOUTHCOM	U.S. Southern Command
WMD	Weapons of Mass Destruction

1. Introduction

Purpose

The Chairman of the Joint Chiefs of Staff (CJCS) and the Joint Staff participate in many Department of Defense (DoD) decisionmaking processes, including crisis response, deliberate operational planning, and fiscally constrained resource and program planning. This participation has become more complex, both because the Goldwater-Nichols Act of 1986 mandated broader CJCS and Joint Staff responsibilities and because the national security environment has become more complicated with the demise of the Soviet Union and reductions in U.S. defense expenditures.

Out of concern that the CJCS and Joint Staff carry out their roles effectively and receive the analytic support necessary to do so, RAND was asked in 1993 to conduct a systematic examination of the Joint Staff's analytic support requirements and its analytic environment and to recommend possible improvements. This report documents the final results of that examination.

Approach

We designed the study as two tasks, together addressing five questions:

Task 1

1. What roles do the CJCS and Joint Staff play in DoD decisionmaking processes, particularly those involving resource identification and allocation?

2. Where do the various Planning, Programming, and Budgeting System (PPBS)-related processes involving the Joint Staff intersect?

3. What is the state of the Joint Staff's current analytic environment, and what information does it require to support well-informed decisionmaking?

Task 2

4. What would an ideal analytic support architecture look like?

5. How easily can existing processes accommodate recommended changes?

The findings from Task 1 were documented in an earlier report,[1] which discussed the roles of the Chairman and the Joint Staff, key formal and informal decisionmaking processes, the Joint Staff's analytic environment and information needs, a proposed analytic support structure, and various organizational considerations. That report observed that the Joint Staff's analytic environment has changed significantly in the 1990s, in several ways:

- The Joint Staff's analytic environment is becoming more complex. It is highly interactive and must provide information and analysis to the Chairman on a wide range of decisions. The complexity is found in the wide range of issues that must be addressed, combined with a plethora of relevant information.

- The tempo of analysis has increased dramatically. The Chairman and the services are frequently expected to provide "quick turnaround" analyses. These requests often stress existing processes, which are structured to produce results based on predetermined timelines that may stretch over two to three years. The Office of the Secretary of Defense (OSD) and Joint Staff members are unanimous in their opinions that the demands for credible "quick turnaround" analyses will increase as the strategic and fiscal environments become more uncertain.

- These analyses are becoming more demanding because they must consider all related factors, such as costs, capabilities, and effectiveness prior to presenting a position.

To improve the Joint Staff's capability for providing the requisite analytic support, we recommended a number of criteria for redefining analytic-support requirements. We also recommended consideration of a possible architecture for satisfying those requirements. This architecture, based on RAND's strategy-to-tasks (STT) decisionmaking framework, develops linkages from the national security strategy to resources.[2] The focus is on DoD-wide capabilities and the

---

[1] Leslie Lewis, John Schrader, James Winnefeld, Richard Kugler, and William Fedorochko, *Analytic Architecture for Joint Staff Decision Support*, RAND, MR-511-JS, 1995.

[2] The strategy-to-tasks methodology (or, in emerging studies, "objective-based planning") was originally developed by Glenn Kent and Ted Warner in the late 1980s. The first study, in 1988, traced requirements for Air Force programs back to the operational and support tasks they were intended to perform and up to the higher-level strategies and objectives the tasks themselves were meant to serve.

Identifying such logical relationships among cascading levels of ends and means provides information necessary both to judge whether the wherewithal exists to achieve the ends and to justify the means as effectively supporting some worthwhile end. Without such knowledge of the logical relationships between means and ends, people can scarcely know whether resources are being allocated effectively or efficiently. (See Edward L. Warner, III and Glenn A. Kent, *A Framework for Planning the Employment of Air Power in Theater War*, RAND, N-2038-AF, 1984. See also, David E. Thaler, *Strategies to Tasks: A Framework for Linking Means and Ends*, RAND, MR-300-AF, 1993.)

resources necessary to support the required capabilities. Its purpose is to provide all participants in resource allocation, management decisions, and analysis a common framework.

An application of RAND's Strategy-to-Tasks Resource Management (STRM) structure to the Joint Staff's unique responsibilities could improve the decisionmaking process by providing decisionmakers with a continuous-thread hierarchical linkage between top-level security objectives and specific DoD programs. The framework could also generate alternative resource cost strategies using quantitative and replicable data. Furthermore, the system would provide an audit trail of resource trade-off options and decisions, a "toolbox" including modeling and databases, as well as personnel with specific expertise to provide additional analytic support.

We also examined organizational changes that should be considered to enable an analytic-support architecture. We outlined several modifications for the Joint Staff to consider:

- Centralizing technology, requirements, and acquisition functions.

- Consolidating the modeling and simulation activities, which would be the underpinnings of the toolbox concept.

- Merging of the exercise program responsibilities into operations.

- Strengthening links between the fiscally constrained strategy functions with force structure and resource assessments.

- Redefining logistics requirements to reflect cross-service and Commander in Chief (CINC) requirements.

Subsequent studies refined and extended the STT framework to decision support for fiscally constrained planning (William Schwabe, C. Robert Roll, Jr., and H. Gary Massey, "Decision Support for Fiscally Constrained Planning Using a Strategies-to-Tasks Approach," unpublished draft), resource allocation and management, (Leslie Lewis and C. Robert Roll, *Strategy-to-Tasks: A Methodology for Resource Allocation and Management*, RAND, P-7839, September 1993. Also, Leslie K. Lewis, James A. Coggin, and C. Robert Roll, "The United States Special Operations Command Resource Management Process: An Application of the Strategy-to-Tasks Framework," unpublished draft), and corporate information management (William Schwabe and Leslie Lewis, *Linking the Corporate Information Management (CIM) Initiative to the Strategy-to-Tasks Framework*, RAND, DB-112-OSD, 1994). The STT framework was used in a variety of studies for U.S. Special Operations Command (USSOCOM), U.S. Forces Korea (USFK), and the Army.

The underlying concept of linking means and ends has remained unchanged through the course of these studies, but the specific entities and their names have varied in different contexts.

Recent Changes in the Joint Staff

Since the Task 1 report (MR-511-JS) was written in late 1993,[3] the Joint Staff has been designated by OSD as a major provider of analyses. In response to this emerging role, the Staff has been reorganized. Many of the suggestions made in the Task 1 report were adopted. Of particular importance is the consolidation of many integration functions under the J-8, which now provides analysis supporting the expanded Joint Requirements Oversight Council (JROC) and many Program Objective Memorandum (POM)-related issues.

Overview of This Report

Figure 1 shows how this report builds on the findings of its predecessor. The left side of the figure shows the sections and content that make up the report on Task 1, and the right side shows the organization of this report. Several changes in the Joint Staff have occurred since the Task 1 report was written; they are described later in this Introduction. Our findings regarding an ideal analytic support architecture (given in Section 2 of this report) build on both the attributes identified earlier (in Section 3 of MR-511-JS) and Joint Staff changes effected since

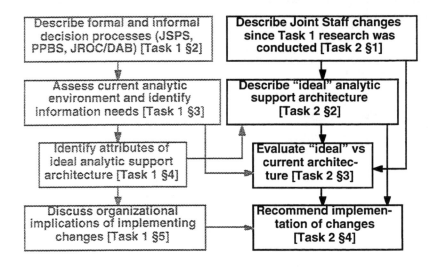

Figure 1—Relationships Between Task 1 and Task 2 Reports

---

[3]In more recent work, RAND is refining the taxonomies and terminology of the strategy-to-tasks approach and refers to the approach as "objective-based planning." See Glenn Kent and William Simons, "Objective-Based Planning," in Paul K. Davis (ed.), *New Challenges for Defense Planning: Rethinking How Much Is Enough*, RAND, Santa Monica, CA, 1994.

then. An evaluation of ideal versus current architecture is given in Section 3 of this report; it builds on the earlier assessment of the current analytic environment and identification of information needs (given in Section 4 of MR-511-JS), Joint Staff changes since then, and the ideal analytic support architecture.

Recommendations for implementation of changes (given in Section 4 of this report) build on the discussion of organizational implications (in Section 5 of the Task 1 report) and the description and evaluation of the ideal architecture.

Appendix A describes more fully the illustrative analytic representation of the U.S. defense posture. Appendices B and C document results of two interactive exercises that were conducted to test concepts of an analytic architecture.

2. An "Ideal" Analytic Support Architecture

The term *analytic architecture* may not be familiar to readers. *Analytic* is used here in the sense of *systems analysis*, which has been defined as "the act, process or profession of studying an activity (as a procedure, a business, or a physiological function) typically by mathematical means in order to define its goals or purposes and to discover operations and procedures for accomplishing them most efficiently."[1] An *architecture* is "a unifying or coherent form or structure" or "the manner in which the components of a . . . system are organized and integrated."[2] Thus, we define an *analytic architecture* for the Joint Staff as *a unifying structure for organizing and integrating studies to help the Chairman discharge his responsibilities effectively and efficiently.*

Figure 2 depicts the current analytic architecture in very general and simple terms. Questions and issues are raised through both formal and informal processes by the Chairman, the Staff itself, CINCs, the services, higher authority, or others. Questions and issues become action items for the Staff if they bear on one or more functions or responsibilities of the Chairman. Analysis to help answer questions or illuminate issues is organized and managed through formal or ad hoc procedures, with varying reliance on management tools. Issues are analyzed using available analytic tools, which range from large, sophisticated computer models to simple, back-of-the-envelope brainstorming. Decisions are then made, and the Chairman or his representatives present military advice and guidance, as appropriate to the function, audience, and medium of communication.

Figure 2—Generalized Depiction of Current Analytic Architecture

---

[1] *Merriam-Webster's Collegiate Dictionary*, Tenth Edition, Merriam-Webster, Incorporated, Springfield, Massachusetts, 1993.

[2] Ibid.

In Task 1 of this study of analytic architecture, we sought to identify a number of existing or in-development architectures that could provide a viable structure and a common tableau. The STT framework was identified, but it was undergoing modifications so it could be more jointly defined than in its original version. In Task 2 we developed strategy-to-tasks further, as part of a more general analytic architecture.

Figure 3 shows the analytic architecture RAND recommends as "ideal." At this level of generality, it is identical to the current architecture but adds one continuing activity: representing the overall defense posture analytically. As shown in the figure, the analytic representation would use the STT framework.

Each part of the architecture is described in some detail, beginning with the analytic representation.

Identification of Questions and Key Issues

Some people would say that the Chairman's most important duty is to raise what are truly the crucial issues for the continuing national security and prosperity of the United States.

Issues are raised through the normal Planning, Programming, and Budgeting System (PPBS) POM process, through the Joint Strategic Planning System (JSPS) JROC process, by CINCs as they prepare their Integrated Priority Lists (IPLs) and testify before Congress, and in response to special interest items from higher authority. One of the ways the Joint Staff commonly seeks to identify key issues and questions is through gaming. For this reason, as part of the evaluation of architectures we conducted two interactive exercises, which included gaming; these are described in Section 3.

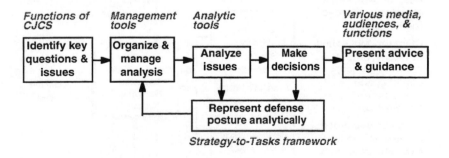

Figure 3—Generalized Depiction of "Ideal" Analytic Architecture

Organization and Management of Analysis

Analysis can be organized and managed in many ways, depending on a host of factors, such as the magnitude, complexity, and urgency of the issues, resources available for the analysis, political or classification sensitivities, and personal styles of management.

Figure 4 shows an example of how a decision node tree can be used to decompose an issue—here the conduct of a major strategy review—using a structured approach to analysis.

This approach clearly represents inputs, outputs, controls (down arrows), and mechanisms (up arrows). A diagram as simple as this one can greatly clarify thinking. In this instance, it shows a frequently overlooked reality—that military strategy, not just programs, is constrained by economic policy and the DoD budget.

Analysis of Issues

Figure 5 suggests some of the analytic tools available to the Joint Staff. A more complete list of existing and needed analytic tools is given in Table 1.

The "tools" vary from computer models (e.g., for costing, tactical simulation, etc.) to systems of administrative and analytic processes (e.g., JSPS), to corporate memory (e.g., lessons-learned reports and databases) to staff with experience and mature judgment. We observed that the use of tools was not consistent across

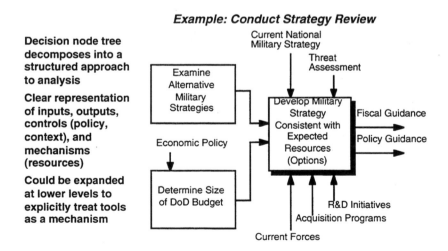

Figure 4—Example of Organizing an Analysis

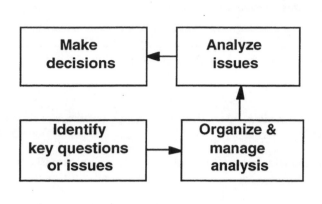

		Tools

Make decisions ← Analyze issues

Identify key questions or issues → Organize & manage analysis ↑ Analyze issues

Tools
- **Micro-costing models**
- **Specialized service specific tactical models**
- **TACWAR and other computer models**
- **Joint Strategic Planning System (JSPS)**
- **Lessons-learned reports**
- **Service-oriented staff experienced with planning factors**
- **Political-military gaming using expert judgment on control teams**
- **Political-military gaming supported by computer models**
- **Review of previous analyses and pol-mil games**

Figure 5—Types of Tools Available to Analyze Issues

areas of analyses. Results from detailed models with many obscure parameters, such as TACWAR, were used for broader policy development activities. There is nothing wrong with application of detailed models or military judgment to many problems; however, the Staff is being asked not only to produce conclusions and options but to demonstrate the analytic underpinning of the analysis. The sophistication and persistence of those asking about such underpinnings are increasing, and the Joint Staff needs better capability to respond.

Figure 6 shows which analytic tools might be appropriate in the illustrative strategy review diagrammed in gross terms in Figure 5. This would be a bottom-up process, ideally an efficient and effective system or network of both series and parallel activities. Interactive planning involves discussions among the principal players either in person or by video-conference.

In addition to the above tools, the concepts and methods of risk analysis can play an important role across many of the CJCS functions. The process of risk analysis involves consideration of both hazard and risk.

"Hazard" is a function of "likelihood of exposure" and "effect of exposure." "Exposure" is readily understood when thinking of toxic agents and may be commonly understood as insurance companies use the term. In some ways the business of the Joint Staff is insurance, and it should be no less interested in

Table 1

Analytic Tools Needed and Existing

CJCS Functions	Needed Tools	Existing Tools
Strategic direction	• Database: studies & key findings (in-house & external)	• Review of previous analyses & pol-mil games
	• Macro-resource models • Pol-mil gaming	• Systems: micro-costing models
Strategic planning	• Pol-mil gaming with quick response campaign models	• Pol-mil gaming using expert judgment of control teams
Contingency planning	• Models to assist existing process	• Joint Strategic Planning System (JSPS)
Requirements, programs, and budgets	• Specialized staff — Conceptual — Joint ops experienced — Analytical • Modeling — Spreadsheet models — High-level cost models — Quick turn capability assessment models	• Service-oriented staff experienced with planning factors • TACWAR model
Joint doctrine, training, & education	• Database: lessons learned keyed to joint operations	• Lessons-learned reports • Gaming
Roles and missions definition	• Campaign-level models with balanced fidelity for joint & combined operations	• Specialized service-specific tactical models

minimizing its exposure to risk than would an insurance company. "Risk" is a function of "hazard" and "perception and valuation." Both can be estimated.

Perception factors include the following:

- Degree of dreadfulness

- How well risk is understood

- Number of people exposed

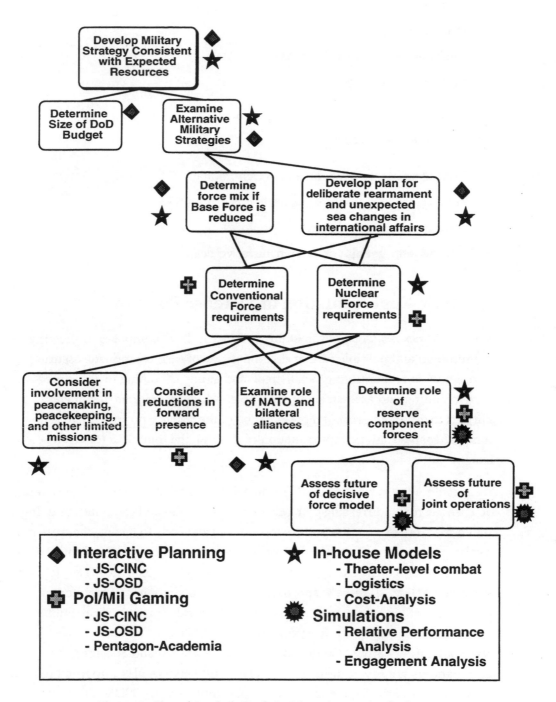

Figure 6—Use of Analytic Tools in Managing an Analysis

Risk can be reduced through any of several interventions, including the following:

- Prevent or reduce the process producing risk
- Reduce exposure

- Modify effects
- Alter perceptions or valuations
- Ameliorate damages

Decisions to reduce risks can be made on the basis of different decision rules, which include the following:

- Utility (maximize net benefits through trade-offs)
- Rights (seek justice, i.e., some trade-offs off-limits)
- Technology (favor advanced technology)
- A priori, e.g., get all you can whenever you can.

Analytic Representation of Defense Posture

An *analytic representation* of something systematically decomposes it, allowing examination and possible further decomposition of each component, assuring completeness or identifying lack thereof, and aiding in coming to a reasoned understanding and assessment of the whole. Although various documents purport to give some sort of representation of the defense posture, there is no comprehensive analytic representation of it within the Joint Staff (or elsewhere in DoD).

Figure 7 shows a variant of the STT framework designed to represent the overall defense posture, addressing both (military) operational and capability-building activities. Considering the posture top-down, from ends to means, there are four levels: policy, operations, assignment, and programming. Responsibilities of the Chairman vary considerably among these levels, as he is likely to (1) advise on or formulate policy, (2) review, approve, or monitor operations, (3) monitor assignment of forces, support, and equipment providing required capabilities, and (4) integrate and prioritize programming. While the Chairman is the principal military advisor at the policy level, the Unified and Specified Commanders are key at the operational level, the services play important roles in assignment, and the Joint Staff shares responsibilities with OSD at the programming level—thus the variance.

As shown in the figure, each of the four levels is decomposed further. Policy includes specifying objectives (sometimes further decomposed into national, national military, and regional military objectives), national and allied interests, and major political, economic, or military constraints. The operational level includes operational strategy, identification of threats or dangers, and

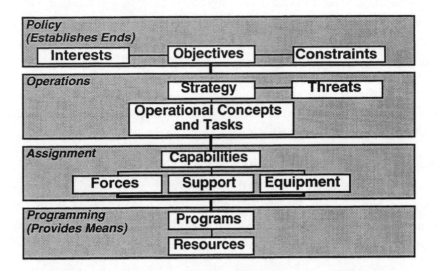

Figure 7—STT Framework for Analytically Representing Defense Posture

operational concepts (interrelated tasks).[3] Assignment includes identification of needed capabilities, as provided by forces, support, and equipment. Programming consists of programs and the resources they require.[4] This report concentrates on the policy and operational levels, but the overall analytic architecture is meant to treat all levels.

The STT framework systematically relates means to ends, to determine if and ensure that (1) appropriate means are available to achieve desired ends and (2) all means can be justified as serving some desired end.

Decisions at the *policy* level establish the desired ends, often called *objectives*, taking into account *threats* (or dangers), national *interests*, *constraints*, and operational *strategy*. At this level, strategy is assumed or given and is not usually itself the subject of analysis. Analysis at this level deals with the best possible identification of threats, interests, and constraints, as well as the best achievable objectives.

---

[3]Operational concepts and tasks can be broken down into a much richer taxonomy involving higher level missions, more concrete operational objectives, and tasks for accomplishing them according to appropriate operational concepts. This will be developed more fully in forthcoming RAND work by Tim Bonds and others.

[4]Figure 7 is not a flow chart, but a requirements and provision chart. Policy establishes the requirements for operations, which provide the wherewithal for making the policy effective. Operations require assignment, and assignment requires programming. Conversely, reading up, resources allow there to be programs, which provide forces, support, and equipment providing capabilities, which enable the performance of operational tasks, and so forth.

At the *operations* level, decisions take objectives, threats, interests, and constraints as given. Analysis at this level deals with the best possible identification of *operational concepts* and subordinate tasks, along with the operational concepts for accomplishing them, yielding the best feasible *strategy*.

Decisions at the *assignment* level take tasks as given. Analysis at this level deals with identification of available forces, *support*, and *equipment* to provide the best *capabilities*, as required by the tasks.

At the *programming* level, decisions take present forces, support, and equipment as given and look ahead to anticipate requirements established at the policy, operations, and assignment levels. Analysis often has to project or predict such requirements and make intertemporal trade-offs, seeking programs that maximize attainment of objectives while minimizing resource costs.

It should be evident that the requirements for analysis *by the Joint Staff* vary by level and entities within a level. For example, at the operational level, it is more essential that the Joint Staff have its own capability to analyze a *strategy* independently of the responsible CINC—to judge whether it will achieve desired objectives within prescribed constraints—than it is to perform equally definitive analysis of individual *tasks*.

STRM is the application of the STT framework to resource management, using a database, spreadsheet, or set of linked diagrams taken down to the program and resource levels.

An actual analytic representation of defense posture created and maintained by the Joint Staff would, of course, be classified and contain otherwise sensitive or restricted information. To illustrate how the defense posture would be analytically represented in practice, RAND researchers used a readily available, unclassified source, the September 1993 report of the Bottom-Up Review (BUR). That version of the BUR mentioned four strategies: (1) Major regional conflicts (MRCs), (2) peace enforcement and intervention, (3) overseas presence, and (4) strategic nuclear.[5] These are represented in Figure 8 within the STT framework.[6]

---

[5] Les Aspin, Secretary of Defense, *The Bottom-Up Review: Forces for a New Era*, Department of Defense, Washington, DC, September 1, 1993.

[6] The BUR treated MRCs and intervention more nearly in a strategy-to-tasks framework than it did for overseas presence and strategic nuclear strategies. Appendix A gives a more complete analytic representation, which RAND developed using MacFlow software on a Macintosh computer. In that environment, a user can browse through the analytic representation by clicking on shadowed boxes, by going directly to subjects of interest, or by searching on key phrases. The format lends itself well to producing Vugraphs, to making extracts for printed reports, and for sharing files with other networked computers. Other similar software is commercially available for various computers.

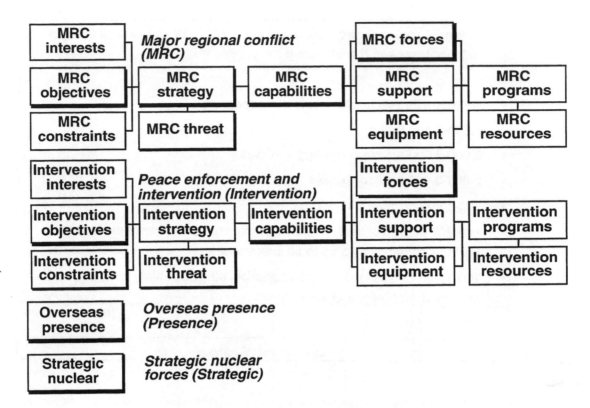

Figure 8—Analytic Representation of Strategies and Related Concepts from the
Bottom-Up Review (BUR)

The shadowed boxes in Figure 8 indicate items, such as the MRC threat, which
are decomposed in further detail.[7] Boxes without shadows in the figure, such as
intervention strategy, are not covered in greater detail. Thus, "holes" in the BUR,
as documented in the September report, are quite evident.

In the MacFlow version of analytic representation, developed for this study,
clicking on the box labeled "MRC threat" causes the information in Figure 9 to be
displayed:

---

[7]The shadowed box convention visually suggests depth or underlying decomposition.
Shadowed boxes are available in several readily available computer application programs, such as
MacFlow and Powerpoint.

Potential regional aggressors are expected to be capable of fielding military forces in the following ranges:

- **400,000-750,000 total personnel under arms**
- **2,000-4,000 tanks**
- **3,000-5,000 armored fighting vehicles**
- **2,000-3,000 artillery pieces**
- **500-1,000 combat aircraft**
- **100-200 naval vessels, primarily patrol craft armed with surface-to-surface missiles, and up to 50 submarines**
- **100-1,000 Scud-class ballistic missiles, some possibly with nuclear, chemical, or biological warheads**

MRC Threat Analysis

Figure 9—Analytic Representation of MRC Threat from BUR

The BUR report gives no MRC threat analysis per se but does give some assumptions about the MRC threat, as shown in the upper two boxes of Figure 10. Given the assumption that North Korea and Iraq are representative of threats from major regional adversaries, some critics of the BUR have said some of the figures in Figure 9 are unrealistically small. Although not stated in the BUR, the lower box of Figure 10 assumes that neither China nor Russia will be adversaries of the United States in a major regional conflict, implied by the numbers in Figure 9. A major advantage of systematically constructing an analytic representation is that it makes so clear what is missing—here, the rationale for some major, conclusion-driving assumptions about threat.

The brief discussion in Figure 10 gives something of the flavor of what could be done in representing the overall defense posture analytically.

Making Decisions

An "ideal" analysis can be thought of as one that yields definitive, credible results. By "definitive" one can mean that it is "the last word." By "credible" one can mean that the results deserve to be believed. In practice, many analyses

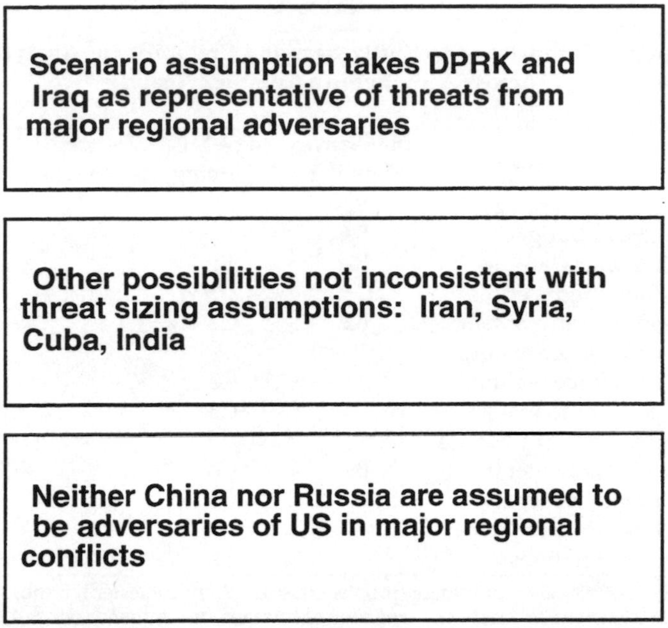

> **Scenario assumption takes DPRK and Iraq as representative of threats from major regional adversaries**

> **Other possibilities not inconsistent with threat sizing assumptions: Iran, Syria, Cuba, India**

> **Neither China nor Russia are assumed to be adversaries of US in major regional conflicts**

Figure 10—Analytic Representation of MRC Threat Analysis from BUR

do not meet rigorous standards with respect to being either definitive or credible. These distinctions are important when it comes to decisionmaking.

Table 2 illustrates how the analytic tools applied at each juncture in an analysis could be rated with respect to expected quality of results, in terms of definitiveness and credibility. Determining military strategy, for example, can be done by interactive planning or pol-mil gaming, with the former being both more definitive and credible. One could imagine an analytic tool that would be the only one available, hence highly definitive, but still lacking in credibility.

It could be helpful in organizing the analysis and planning for management of decisionmaking to estimate the levels of definitiveness and credibility likely to result from each analytic activity. These estimates could be revised as analytic activities are completed and briefed.

Decisionmaking is the responsibility of senior military leadership, ultimately, within the Joint Staff, the Chairman. An ideal analytic support architecture would give support, not make the decisions. It would, however, record the decisions, to provide an audit trail and facilitate future work; this could be done through updating the analytic representation of the defense posture.

Table 2

**Illustrative Estimates of Definitiveness and Credibility of Analytic Tools
Across Activities in a Complex Analysis**

Activity	Interactive Planning	Pol-Mil Gaming	In-House Models	Simulations
Determine military strategy	B2	C3		
Determine size of budget	B2			
Examine alternate strategies	B2	B2		
Determine mix if reduced	C3	C3		
Develop plan for rearmament	B2	C3		
Determine conv. force req'mts			C3	
Determine nuc. force req'mts		C3		B2
Consider ops other than war		C3		
Consider reduced fwd presence			C3	
Examine NATO & bilaterals	B3	C3		
Determine role of reserves		C3	C3	C3
Assess future of decisive force			C3	C3
Assess future of joint ops			C3	C3

NOTES: *Definitiveness* of framing problem/issues: A (uncontested), B (near-consensus), C (adequate), D (deficient), F (useless). *Credibility* of findings/recommendations: 1 (uncontested), 2 (near-consensus), 3 (adequate), 4 (deficient), 5 (useless).

Presenting Advice and Guidance

Presentation of military advice and guidance by the Chairman or his representatives should and does vary by audience, content, and medium of communication. The value of maintaining a comprehensive, structured analytic representation lies, in part, in its utility as a "mine" of information, which can be exploited and processed further for nearly any presentation.

3. Evaluation of Analytic Support Architectures

Characteristics of Joint Staff Analysis

Many organizations, including the Joint Staff, are tempted to believe that the world revolves around them, that it is they who do *everything*. In fact, it is impossible for the Joint Staff to do all the analysis required to support all the issues and decisions facing the Chairman. Much of the analysis used by the Joint Staff is externally produced by CINCs, the services, other agencies, contractors, or others; this is how it should be and must be. What, then, are the responsibilities of the Joint Staff with respect to externally produced analysis? Is there, in fact, analysis that can or should be done by only the Joint Staff?

Figure 11 shows characteristics that are distinctive of analysis done by the Joint Staff. With respect to externally produced analysis, the Joint Staff has both Quality Assurance (QA) and Quality Control (QC) responsibilities. QA takes the form of various guidance given by the Chairman to CINCs, services, and others suggesting what analysis to do and how to do it. QC reviews, assesses, verifies, or validates externally conducted work in progress or upon completion. It may take the form of reviewing the logic in a report, error checking, or independently replicating or verifying the analysis. QC may or may not, in itself, be analysis. Integrative analysis takes the results of externally or other internally produced analysis and "puts it together." This is done to show a larger picture, make

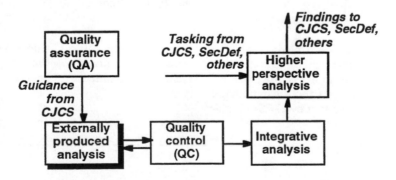

Figure 11—Distinctive Characteristics of Joint Staff Analysis

trade-offs among mutually exclusive demands, assumptions, or findings, resolve inconsistencies, or "fill holes" among analyses. Finally, there is analysis from a broader perspective than that of a service, CINC, or particular community. Tasking for such analysis often comes from the Chairman or higher authority.

Table 3 summarizes our evaluation of the current analytic architecture in practice, its potential, and the proposed "ideal" architecture, regarding QA, QC, integrative analysis, and broader perspective analysis.

Table 3

Comparison of Current, Current Potential, and Ideal Architectures with Respect to Types of Analysis Distinctive to the Joint Staff

Type of Analysis	Current in Practice	Current Potential	Ideal
QA	Good. Much useful guidance is given, but external analysts must often assume concrete policies or priorities beyond what CJCS provides.	Very good. Viewing guidance as quality assurance and adopting QA practices from the private sector could improve on current practice.	Excellent. Analytic representation could provide better understanding of deficiencies and insufficiencies.
QC	Fair. Some analyses are not reviewed critically by Joint Staff analysts. There are no uniformly applied standards for analysis, though there are for some briefings of results.	Good, if this function were taken more seriously. Triage concept could be applied, differentiating among good-as-is, needs improvement, and beyond redemption analyses.	Excellent. Having an analytic representation as a starting point or baseline would simplify and otherwise lessen QC work required.
Integrative	Fair. Leaves much to be desired.	Fair-to-good. Improvement dependent on development of new standards or techniques.	Excellent. Common framework would greatly simplify and otherwise improve integration.
Broader	Fair-to-excellent. Highly dependent on caliber of personnel assigned to analysis and the importance given to it by CJCS or higher authority.	Fair-to-excellent. Little different from current architecture in practice.	Good-to-excellent. Broader perspective analysis would rest on a stronger base of quality controlled and integrated analysis.

Identifying Key Issues for Analysis

As has been explained, the RAND concept of an analytic architecture would use an analytic representation of the overall defense posture as a baseline regarding key issues that might be raised and examined.

There is a school of thought that current processes are quite adequate for bringing the important issues to the fore and resolving them. Certainly the system does work well in many—perhaps most—instances. It may indeed be the best to be hoped for, given the environment of political rivalries and military uncertainties.

Nevertheless, discussions with current and former senior officials have suggested a number of areas for improvement; several were discussed in the earlier companion report (MR-511-JS). To evaluate possible benefits of the proposed analytic architecture solely to raise and address key issues for analysis, we conducted a research game consisting of two moves, each dealing with a single, simply stated scenario. Two teams deliberated independently, working the same problem; on completion of deliberations, each presented and discussed its decisions, rationale, and expectations.

Players found the single most useful information based on the analytic representation was that shown in Figure 12, which suggests some of the issues the Korean scenario might raise, superimposed on an analytic representation of

RAND*MR651-12*

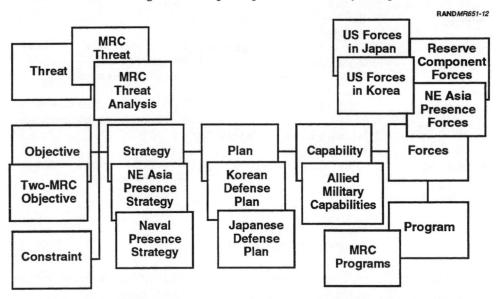

Figure 12—Use of Analytic Representation to Suggest Issues Korean Reunification Might Raise

the MRC strategy and related concepts. Development of such a diagram in a brainstorming session could itself be a useful device for surfacing key issues.

Table 4 suggests how the issues raised by players on both teams can be represented analytically.

Evaluating Analysis of Issues: The Example of Overseas Presence

The second exercise was hosted by RAND in support of ongoing Joint Staff (J-5) coordination of the Joint Warfighting Capabilities Assessment (JWCA) panel dealing with overseas presence issues.[1]

Table 4

Analytic Representation of Issues Raised in Korean Scenario

Analytic Concept	Team A Issues	Team B Issues
Interests	Is this a successful outcome? Is this a favorable situation?	How does this affect defense interests?
Objectives	Will this change the focus of foreign policy? Do objectives in Asia-Pacific change?	
Constraints		How will this affect Japanese? Will unified Korea be ROK or new state?
Strategy	Will this change national military strategy? How to hedge against adverse change in Korea? Does strategy need to be presented differently?	How to hedge against adverse change in Korea? Should CJCS rearticulate U.S. military strategy?
Threats	What is the current threat in Korea? Is there other rationale for U.S. troops in Korea?	How does this affect threats? Will Korea be a nuclear power?
Operational Concepts and Tasks, Capabilities, Forces	Where should forces redeploy?	What should be done with forces now in Korea?
Equipment Support Programs	Does this change active/ reserve/guard roles/mix?	
Resources	Will this affect level of defense spending?	What actions needed in dealing with Congress?

---

[1] Appendix B provides additional details on the overseas presence workshop.

Participants in the workshop were not sufficiently familiar with the proposed analytic architecture or skilled in the use of the analytic tools it would employ actually to use or to test the architecture. RAND analysts concluded that the issues identified by participants during game deliberations and other discussions could productively be organized, represented, and analyzed using the architecture, but this would more appropriately be done by Joint Staff analysts rather than action officers or senior decisionmakers.

A Philosophy of Evaluation

Good analysis is logical, its findings and recommendations are logical, and a defense posture developed on the basis of such analysis should be logical: reasonable, consistent, plausible, sufficiently complete, exhaustive, and detailed so as to be sensible. All operations of our government, including analysis, are meant to be ethical: honest, responsible, accountable, and done with integrity. Analysis and the processes by which analyses are conducted, administered, and evaluated should be fair: with respect given to and understanding of differing interests' points of view, responsive to the needs of those having a stake in it, and accommodating to special or changed circumstances.

Attributes of Analytic Architecture

The desirable attributes of an analytic support architecture, largely as identified in Section 4 of the Task 1 report, can be understood in the framework of logic, ethics, and fairness:

Logic

- Link concepts, assumptions, and facts logically to provide a common framework across all decision processes
- Support integration functions across services and regions[2]
- Present a structured, coherent view of all elements going into determining military capabilities
  — Show hierarchy of linkages from national security strategy and national military strategy down to specific DoD programs

[2]Although the current emphasis on jointness is intended to promote integration across services, integration across geographic regions is not so explicitly stated as a goal of the Joint Staff.

- — Accommodate and help structure inputs, analytic processes, and outputs of formal processes and ad hoc analyses
- — Provide consistent, common tableau for viewing an issue[3]
- — Generate alternatives to plans or costs, to address effectiveness and cost trade-off issues across operational objectives
- — Motivate end-to-end concept of operations development, ensuring that related issues, such as readiness and sustainability, are addressed
- — Be sufficiently quantitative and replicable so that an audit trail of decisions can be reviewed as guidance changes
- — Acknowledge and, to the extent possible, address risks, uncertainties, unknowns, and the potential effects of each.

Ethics

- • Reflect Chairman's independent advice to SecDef and President

Fairness

- • Accommodate formal, informal, and ad hoc analytic requirements

- • Accommodate all types of data demanded

- • Be sufficiently structured to work in any domain, i.e., across a wide range of types of decisions and alternatives

- • Be understandable and accepted by CINCs, services, and OSD

- • Allow all players to participate in processes

Based on the games and the foregoing discussion, Table 5 summarizes our evaluation of the current analytic architecture in practice, its potential, and the proposed "ideal" architecture, with respect to the criteria of logic, ethics, and fairness.

---

[3]For example, standards for presenting information to the JROC provide a common format or tableau that facilitates logically consistent thinking about trade-offs.

Table 5

**Comparison of Current and Ideal Architectures with Respect
to Desirable Attributes of Joint Staff Analysis**

Attribute	Current	Ideal
Provide common framework across resource decision processes	No	Yes
Support cross-service cross-region integration	Inadequate	Good
Present structured, coherent elements of capabilities	No	Good
Reflect Chairman's independent advice	Yes	Yes
Accommodate formal, informal, and ad hoc analytic requirements	Yes	Yes
Accommodate all types of data demanded	No	Yes
Be sufficiently structured to work in any domain	No	Yes
Be understandable and accepted by CINCs, services, and OSD	Relatively well understood and somewhat accepted	Thoroughly understood and well accepted
Allow all players to participate in processes	Yes	Yes

4. Implementation of Changes

CJCS Responsibilities and Information Needs

In an October 1993 briefing[1] the Joint Staff identified the following responsibilities of the Chairman, as specified in Title 10 United States Code (USC), noting in parentheses the processes and documents responding:

- Assisting the National Command Authority in providing strategic direction (*National Military Strategy* (NMS))

- Strategic planning
  - Prepare strategic plans (*Joint Strategic Capabilities Plan* (JSCP))
  - Prepare joint logistic and mobility plans to support strategic plans (JSCP)
  - Perform net assessments to determine capabilities (*CJCS Program Assessment* (CPA))[2]

- Contingency planning; preparedness
  - Provide for the preparation and review of contingency plans (JSCP)
  - Prepare joint logistic and mobility plans to support contingency plans (JSCP)
  - Advise the Secretary of Defense (SecDef) on critical deficiencies and strengths in force capabilities identified during preparation and review of contingency plans and assess their effect on meeting national security objectives (*Preparedness Assessment Report* (PAR))
  - Establish and maintain, in consultation with CINCs, a uniform system of evaluating the preparedness of each command to carry out assigned missions (Preparedness Evaluation System (PES): *CINC's Preparedness Assessment Report* (CSPAR) and PAR *Logistics Sustainability Analysis* (LSA))

- Advice on requirements, programs, and budget
  - Advise SecDef on priorities of requirements identified by CINCs (CPA)

---

[1] "Are Our Planning & Programming Systems Responsive?" Prepared by the Joint Staff, J-7 in collaboration with J-3, J-4, J-5 & J-8 (6 October 1993).

[2] Title 10 also requires the Secretary of Defense to submit to Congress an annual net assessment. The Joint Military Net Assessment (JMNA), which is prepared by the CJCS, responds to this requirement.

— Advise SecDef on extent to which programs and budget proposals (services and other DoD components) conform with priorities established in strategic plans and priorities established for requirements of the CINCs (CPA) (*Joint Planning Document* (JPD))
— Submit to SecDef alternative program recommendations and budget proposals to achieve greater conformance with priorities (CPA) (Processes of Issue Papers and *Program Budget Decisions* (PBDs))
— Assess military requirements for defense acquisition programs (JROC)

That's a lot to have on anyone's plate—a lot of things to keep consistent with one another and be accessible. To integrate all these documents—making sure that decisions are logically, ethically, and fairly arrived at—there is need for one, overarching approach.

Our Task 1 report identified a need to provide structure to planning, programming, and budgeting decision processes, shown in Table 6 as semi-structured or unstructured.

OSD and Joint Staff processes are not unrelated to one another, but the relationships among their functions and products are not particularly clear, and both processes and relationships may be less than optimal. The STT framework can provide structure that is useful in understanding the separate processes and relationships among processes. That understanding includes (1) the rationale "horizontally" relating operational dependencies among tasks (the *end-to-end* concept) and "vertically" relating ends to means (objectives to strategy to tasks to programs to resources) and (2) the level and type of analysis appropriate to each function and product. Such understanding can (1) help identify issues and requirements and (2) improve organizational efficiency and effectiveness. Implementation of the recommendations can be made incrementally or less conservatively, as circumstances may warrant.

The Expanded JROC

Recently, the Vice Chairman has expanded the role of the JROC, as an important vehicle for increasing U.S. military efficiency and effectiveness through jointness. Thus, an example of implementing the proposed analytic architecture in the JROC may be especially useful. The following discussion is independent of the ongoing JWCA process but is not inconsistent with it.[3]

---

[3]JWCA integration and input to the JROC will be addressed in a forthcoming RAND report.

Table 6

Information Needed to Support the CJCS

Type of Information	Decision Process		
	Planning	Programming	Budgeting
Structured	(JSPS) Strategic directions	New assessments	Assess impact of budget issues on military capabilities
	Military strategy	CINC requirements	
	Risk evaluation	Program review	
	Scenarios	Options	
		CJCS program assessment	
		Evaluate acquisition programs	
Semi-structured	New threat	Assist in new budget guidance	Revise force structure to fiscal guidance
	Revised planning guidance	Revise force structure	Revise modernization and acquisition programs
	New capability planning	Assist in revising fiscally constrained planning factors	Provide force structure and cost alternatives
Unstructured	New scenarios	Revise modernization & acquisition plan	
	Short-term forecasting	R&D planning Assist in revised program plan	

The JROC makes decisions at several points along the major systems acquisition process. The first decision is whether to approve a given Mission Need Statement (MNS). Decision briefings presented to the JROC are generally structured as shown in Figure 13.[4]

This is basically a good structure for presentation of a mission need by an advocate to the JROC, but we recommend two ways in which the analytic architecture might usefully be implemented here.

---

[4] Adapted from *JROC Briefing Guide*, JROCM-049-92, 6 July 1992.

MISSION NEED STATEMENT

PURPOSE
> MNS validation

SUMMARIZED THREAT/NATIONAL DEFENSE POLICY
> Threat to be countered
> Projected threat environment

STATE REQUIRED CAPABILITIES (Identifies needs)

NONMATERIEL SOLUTIONS EXAMINED
> Change in doctrine
> Change in operational concepts
> Change in tactics
> Change in training/education
> Change in organization (force structure)

COMPARISON PROCESS (Need versus existing capabilities)

WHAT ARE THE ISSUES

RECOMMENDATION (What briefer wants the JROC to do)

Figure 13—Current Structure of Mission Need Statement

The first is to add (a) more explicit vertical linkage up the strategy-to-tasks chain, to identify which ends the proposed means would meet and (b) explicit horizontal end-to-end linkage, to identify how the proposed capability would be used by CINCs in new or existing operational concepts. These additions are shown in bold in Figure 14.

The second improvement is to require that an independent Joint Staff assessment be briefed in addition to that presented by the advocate. It would explicitly assess how well ends are met by present and projected capabilities, comparing this with an assessment of how well ends would be met given the proposed capabilities. The assessment would also suggest what else might be needed, what might be eliminated, and the effects of the proposed capabilities on joint and allied interoperability. Attention could be given to hedges against uncertain threats, system performance, and so forth.

Were the analytic architecture to be successfully and usefully implemented in this fashion in the JROC, it would also spread to the services (who are generally the advocates for mission needs statements) and the Joint Staff (who would be using it in preparing independent assessments).

MISSION NEED STATEMENT

PURPOSE
  Mission need statement validation
SUMMARIZED THREAT/NATIONAL DEFENSE POLICY
  Threat to be countered
  Projected threat environment
  Defense policy (ends) to be supported
STATE REQUIRED CAPABILITIES (Identifies needs)
NONMATERIEL SOLUTIONS EXAMINED
  Change in doctrine
  Change in operational concepts
  Change in tactics
  Change in training/education
  Change in organization (force structure)
COMPARISON PROCESS (Need versus existing capabilities)
  Comparison with other systems
  Comparison with other operational concept(s)
WHAT ARE THE ISSUES
RECOMMENDATION (What briefer wants the JROC to do)

Figure 14—Proposed Structure of Mission Need Statement

More generally, STRM appears to have the following strengths and limitations:

- STRENGTHS
  - Links national security objectives to resources
  - Provides a common tableau for the assessment and discussion of joint capabilities
  - Links force structure and equipment to capabilities
  - Provides a framework in which options can be generated and debated
  - Is consistent with the resource decision process
  - Enables decisionmakers to generate trade-offs among the services.

- LIMITATIONS
  - Does not contain models or assumptions about relative importance among objectives
  - Requires external development of operational concepts
  - Must be revalidated when major assumptions change
  - Must be used cautiously to avoid claiming that because of links across levels everything in the hierarchy is linked to everything else.

Joint Warfighting Capabilities Assessments Integration

Figure 15 shows the cross-walk between the JWCA groups and STRM.

As shown, the STRM Joint Operational Tasks (JOTs) are the building blocks for assessing how well forces can support achieving objectives. Issues are developed in individual JWCAs (or in ad hoc combinations such as Intelligence, Surveillance, and Reconnaissance (ISR)/Strike consortiums for precision strike analysis), but they need to be presented in the context of the national objective that they support.

Figure 16 (an extract from the STRM database) shows how some selected STRM JOTs can be used as an integration tool spanning the range of JWCA functional areas and groups. Each task requires capability assessments from the perspective of one or more JWCAs. The analysis can be performed by bringing JWCAs together or by identifying non-overlapping subtasks and building an overall integrated assessment from the component pieces.

The expanded JROC activities with their supporting JWCAs are evidence of the increasing demand for analysis anticipated in the first phase of this study. Organizing the evolving analytic capabilities of the Joint Staff, services, CINCs,

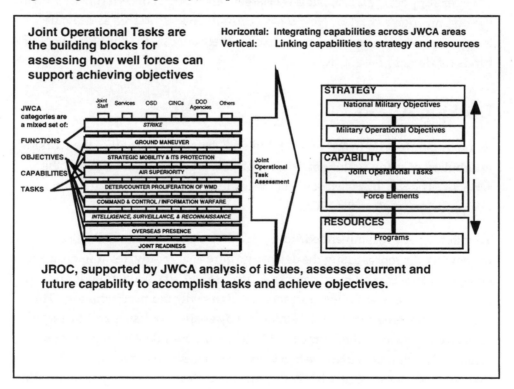

Figure 15—Cross-Walk from JWCA to STRM

RANDMR651-16

4	**Joint Operational Tasks** Assessment criteria: ability to perform task based on constituent force elements' capability (number; active/reserve; equipment; organization)										
							JWCA				
Ref. No.	Description	Strike	Gnd Man- euver	Strat Mob & Protection	Air Sup	Deter/ Counter Prolif	C2 Info Warf	ISR	Over- seas Pres	Joint Readi- ness
62	Participate in arms control treaty implementation					X				
63	Destroy hardware and munitions					X		X		
64	Monitor proliferation					X		X		
65	Verify implementation of agreements					X	X	X		
66	Retaliate with nuclear weapons					X	X	X		
67	Retaliate with conventional weapons	X				X	X	X		
76	Ensure compliance with cease-fire agreements	X	X		X		X	X		
77	Destroy enemy WMD in storage areas	X				X	X	X		
83	Support defense unique industries and technologies									X
84	Negotiate/monitor agreements for access and overflight rights								X	

Figure 16—STRM JOTs and Related JWCA Functional Areas

and supporting contractors is a daunting task that should be simplified by incorporating the analytic framework developed in this paper. When the project began, the leadership of J-8 was concerned with developing a model for analysis to better support the CJCS, but it was largely an internal concern consistent with the organization's charter. Now the concerns are widely shared as difficult integration decisions must be made to effectively allocate the shrinking pool of funds for defense programs.

Looking Ahead

By now, "strategy-to-tasks" and "end-to-end" have become part of the working vocabulary of many senior officials in OSD, the Joint Chiefs of Staff, and the services. The STT framework would be relatively easy to introduce into some key processes, such as the JROC.

To reiterate, our recommended "ideal" architecture is an expanded STT framework for representing the defense posture analytically, relating means to ends, to ensure that all means and ends are justified. It considers ends and means at four levels: policy, operations, assignment, and programming. This analytic representation would be informed by analysis of issues and by records of decisions made by the Secretary of Defense, the President, Congress, and others. The analytic representation would be an input to organizing and managing analysis. Similarly, Strategy-to-Tasks Resource Management (STRM) can be applied as a database to aid the Joint Staff in analysis. In addition, an "analytic toolbox" is suggested to aid the Joint Staff in undertaking analysis.

These analytic tools include databases, political-military gaming, models, spreadsheets, and lessons learned.

Among the changes for the Joint Staff to consider are the following:

- Centralize technology, requirements, and acquisition functions.

- Consolidate the modeling and simulation activities, which would be the underpinnings of the toolbox concept.

- Merge the exercise program responsibilities into operations.

- Strengthen links between the fiscally constrained strategy functions with force structure and resource assessments.

- Refine logistics requirements to reflect cross-service and Commander in Chief requirements.

Appendix
A. Analytic Representation of Defense Posture

We used the September 1993 BUR as the basis for illustrating analytic representation of the defense posture. The software used for this application was MacFlow, which has provision for nested flowcharts. Alternatively, the analytic representation can be implemented using a spreadsheet, such as Excel, or a relational database, such as FoxPro, either on a Macintosh or PC computer.

Figure A.1 is a strategy-to-tasks overview of the analytic representation. The boxes with shadows (Objectives, Constraints, Strategy, Threats, Operational concepts and tasks, Forces, Capabilities, and Programs) have associated with them nested information. On-line, using MacFlow, one accesses such information by double-clicking on a shadowed box. The boxes without shadows are not now supported by further nested information. Lack of shadows readily shows incompleteness.

Working on a computer, one can navigate through any of several paths, depending on one's interests. To illustrate here, a single path through part of the overall representation is shown through a series of figures.

Figure A.2 shows the *Objectives* given in the September 1993 BUR.[1] Double-clicking on *Enduring U.S. goals* brings up the information shown in Figure A.3.

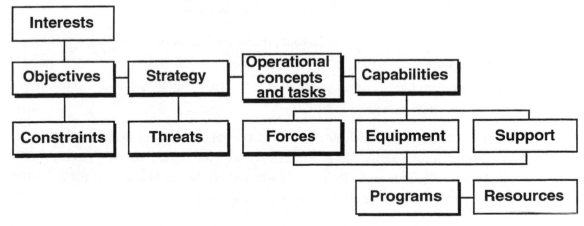

Figure A.1—Overview

[1]Les Aspin, Secretary of Defense, *The Bottom-Up Review: Forces for a New Era*, Department of Defense, Washington, DC, September 1, 1993.

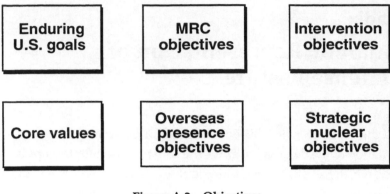

| Enduring U.S. goals | MRC objectives | Intervention objectives |
| Core values | Overseas presence objectives | Strategic nuclear objectives |

Figure A.2—Objectives

Protect the lives and personal safety of Americans, both at home and abroad

Provide for the well-being and prosperity of the nation and its people

Maintain the political freedom and independence of the United States with its values, institutions, and territory intact

Figure A.3—Enduring U.S. Goals

Clicking on *Core values* displays what is shown in Figure A.4, and clicking on *MRC objectives* displays Figure A.5.

The MRC objective includes a statement of the rationale for dealing with two nearly simultaneous MRCs. The implications for capabilities refers to the *MRC building block* concept. There is a shadowed symbol that can access the definition of the MRC building block, as shown in Figure A.6.

> Democracy and
> human rights

> Peaceful resolution of
> conflict

> Maintenance of open
> markets in the
> international
> economic system

Figure A.4—Core Values

RAND*MR651-A.5*

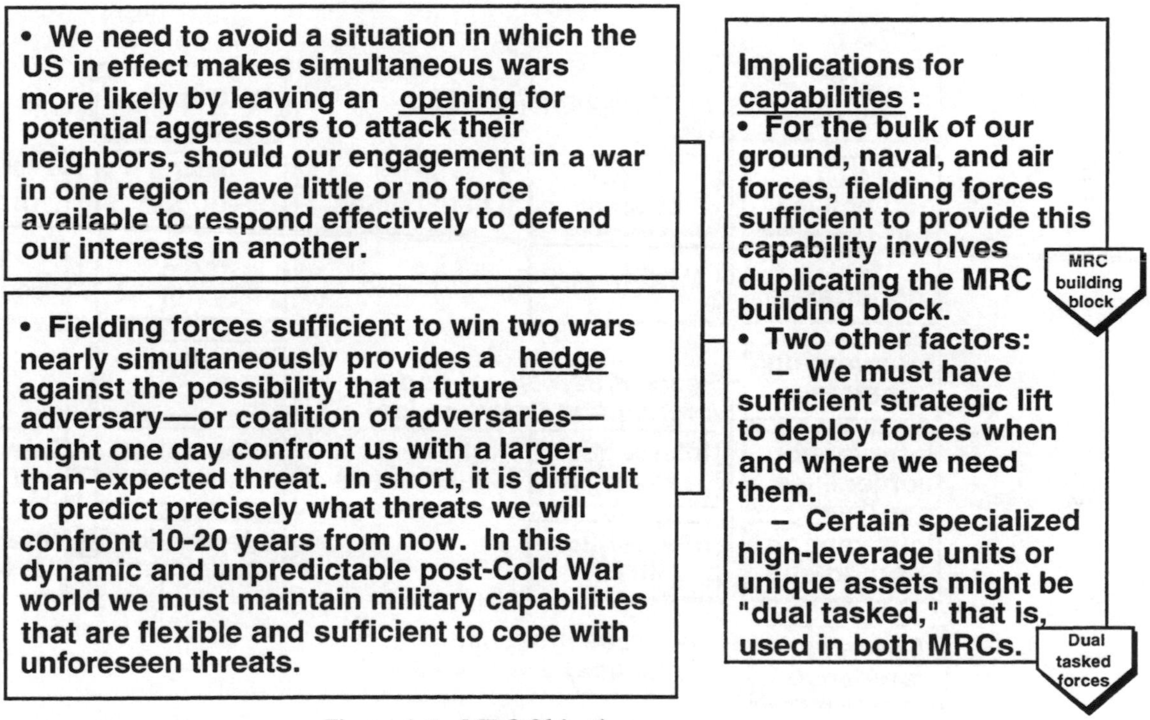

- We need to avoid a situation in which the US in effect makes simultaneous wars more likely by leaving an <u>opening</u> for potential aggressors to attack their neighbors, should our engagement in a war in one region leave little or no force available to respond effectively to defend our interests in another.

- Fielding forces sufficient to win two wars nearly simultaneously provides a <u>hedge</u> against the possibility that a future adversary—or coalition of adversaries—might one day confront us with a larger-than-expected threat. In short, it is difficult to predict precisely what threats we will confront 10-20 years from now. In this dynamic and unpredictable post-Cold War world we must maintain military capabilities that are flexible and sufficient to cope with unforeseen threats.

Implications for capabilities :
- For the bulk of our ground, naval, and air forces, fielding forces sufficient to provide this capability involves duplicating the MRC building block.
- Two other factors:
  – We must have sufficient strategic lift to deploy forces when and where we need them.
  – Certain specialized high-leverage units or unique assets might be "dual tasked," that is, used in both MRCs.

> MRC
> building
> block

> Dual
> tasked
> forces

Figure A.5—MRC Objectives

If, instead of double-clicking on *Objectives* in the display shown in Figure A.1, one were to click on *Strategy*, the information shown in Figure A.7 would be displayed. Here, in fact, we see several strategies—*MRC strategy, Intervention strategy,* and several others—each shown in a top-down strategy-to-tasks framework. Double-clicking on *MRC strategy* displays the information shown in Figure A.8.

The following forces will be adequate to execute the strategy for a single MRC:

- **4-5 Army divisions**
- **4-5 Marine Expeditionary Brigades**
- **10 Air Force fighter wings**
- **100 Air Force heavy bombers**
- **4-5 Navy aircraft carrier battle groups**
- **Special operations forces**

MRC force: military judgment

Figure A.6—MRC Building Block

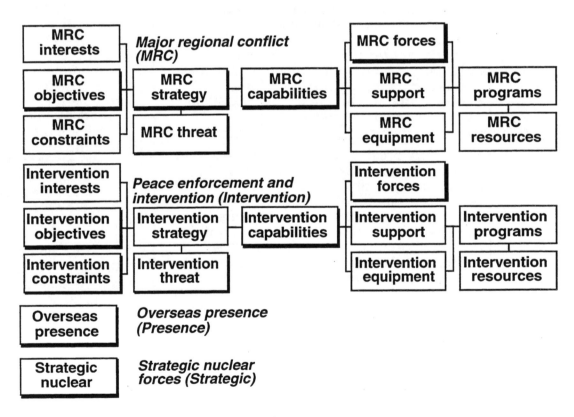

Figure A.7—Strategy

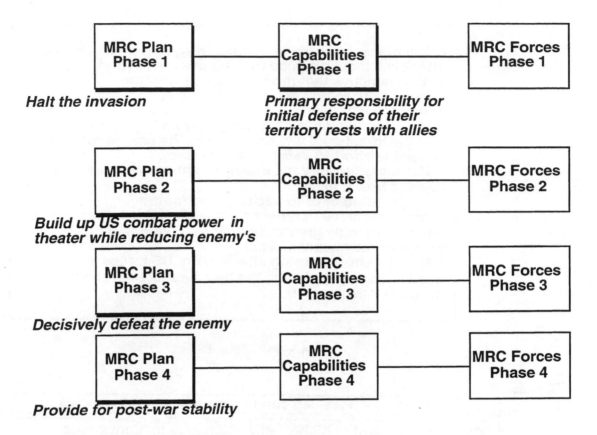

Figure A.8—MRC Strategy

The BUR MRC strategy calls for a four-phase MRC campaign plan, giving information on planning assumptions for each phase but referring to capabilities only for phase 1. The phase 1 planning assumptions are shown in Figure A.9, and the capabilities in Figure A.10.

Figure A.10 shows capabilities to the left and associated forces to the right.

Under capabilities, there is no mention of protecting friendly forces and rear-area assets from attack by enemy special operations forces (SOF). Under forces, there could be added ground fire support units to delay, disrupt, and destroy enemy ground forces, C^3I forces to locate high-value targets, and bombers to help establish maritime superiority.[2]

If, working from the overview display shown in Figure A.1, one were to double-click on *Capabilities*, another menu would be displayed, which could be used to access aspects of *MRC capabilities*, as shown in Figure A.11.

_____

[2]These additions were suggested by RAND colleague Bruce Bennett.

- The highest priority in defending against a large-scale attack will most often be to minimize the territory and critical facilities that the invader can capture.
- Should strategic assest fall to the invader, it might attempt to use them as bargaining chips.
- Stopping the invasion quickly may be key to ensuring that the threatened ally can continue its crucial role in the collective effort to defeat the aggressor.
- The more territory the enemy captures, the greater the price to take it back
  - The number of forces required for the counteroffensive to repel an invasion can increase, with correspondingly greater casualties, depending on the progress the enemy makes.
- Given a short-warning attack, more US forces would need to deploy rapidly to the theater and enter the battle as quickly as possible.

Figure A.9—MRC Plan: Phase 1

Forces of beseiged country move to blunt the attack	
Rapid deployment of highly lethal US forces to blunt attack	
US Capabilities	*US Forces*
Help allied forces establish viable defense to halt enemy ground forces before they achieve critical objectives	Combination of land- and sea-based strike aircraft, heavy bombers, long-range tactical missiles, ground maneuver forces with antiarmor capabilities, and special operations forces
Delay, disrupt, & destroy enemy ground forces; damage roads on which they are moving, to halt attack	
Protect friendly forces & rear-area assets from attack by aircraft or cruise and ballistic missiles	Land and sea-based aircraft, ground- and sea-based surface-to-air missiles, and special operations forces
Establish air superiority and suppress enemy air defenses as needed, including those in rear areas and accompanying invading ground forces	Land- and sea-based strike and jamming aircraft; surface-to-surface missiles, such as ATACMS
Destroy high-value targets, such as WMD, and degrade enemy's ability to prosecute military operations through attacks focused on his central C3 facilities	Long-range bombers, land and sea-based strike aircraft, cruise missiles, and special operations forces
Establish maritime superiority, to ensure access to ports and sea LOCs and as a precondition for amphibious assaults	Naval task forces with mine countermeasure ships

Figure A.10—MRC Capabilities: Phase 1

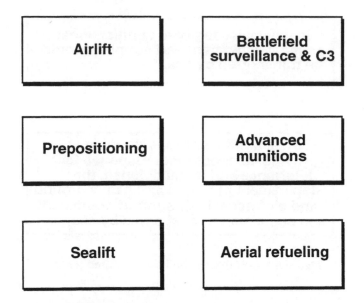

Figure A.11—Capabilities Required for MRC

Double-clicking on *Airlift* displays the information shown in Figure A.12, on *Sealift* that shown in Figure A.13.

Battlefield surveillance and C3 is shown in Figure A.14. The list of forces is incomplete in that no forces are shown supporting the first three capabilities.

As is evident, many paths through the analytic representation are possible. Returning to the *Strategy* display shown in Figure A.7, double-clicking on *Intervention forces* would display the information shown in Figure A.15.

• **Adequate airlift capacity is needed to bring in forces and materiel required for the first weeks of an operation.**

• **In Operations Desert Shield and Storm US delivered on average more than 2,400 tons of material per day by airlift; at least the same level of lift capacity is anticipated to support high-intensity military operations in the opening phase of a future MRC and to help sustain operations thereafter**

Figure A.12—Airlift Capabilities Required for MRC

- In any major regional conflict, most combat equipment and supplies would be transported by sea.

- While airlift and prepositioning provide the most rapid response for deterrence and initial defense, the deployment of significant heavy ground and air forces, their support equipment, and sustainment must come by sea.

Figure A.13—Sealift Capabilities Required for MRC

Capabilities   **Forces**

- Accurate information on the location and disposition of enemy forces is a prerequisite for effective military operations.

- Our planning envisions the early deployment of reconnaissance and C2 aircraft and ground-based assets to enable our forces to see the enemy and to pass information quickly through all echelons of our forces.

- Total US intelligence and surveillance capability will be less than it was during the Cold War, but it will be better able to provide timely information to battlefield commanders.

Joint Surveillance and Target Attack Radar System (JSTARS), the upgraded Airborne Warning and Control System (AWACS), and the MILSTAR satellite communications system

- Advanced systems will ensure that US forces have a decisive advantage in tactical intelligence and communications.

Figure A.14—Battlefield Surveillance and C3

> **The prudent level of forces that should be planned for a major intervention or peace enforcement operation is:**
>
> 1 air assault or airborne division
> 1 light infantry division
> 1 Marine Expeditionary Brigade
> 1-2 carrier battle groups
> 1-2 composite wings of Air Force aircraft
> Special operations forces
> Civil affairs units
> Airlift and sealift forces
> Combat support and service support units
>
> ---
>
> **50,000 total combat and support personnel**

Figure A.15—Intervention Forces

Double-clicking from the *Strategy* display on *Overseas presence* would call up the information shown in Figure A.16. Clicking on *Northeast Asian presence* displays Figure A.17; from there, clicking on *NE Asian presence forces* brings up Figure A.18.

Combat Support (CS) and Combat Service Support (CSS) forces are not listed.

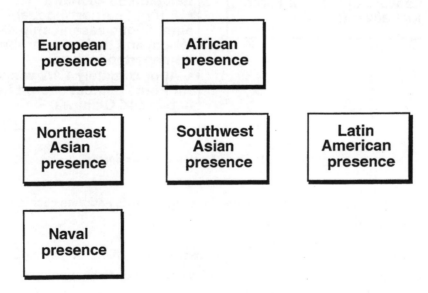

Figure A.16—Overseas Presence

44

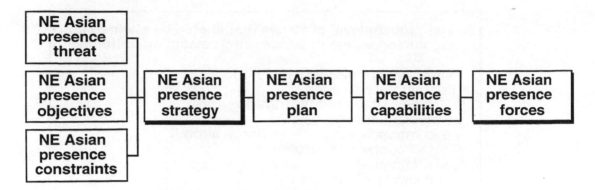

Figure A.17—Northeast Asian Presence

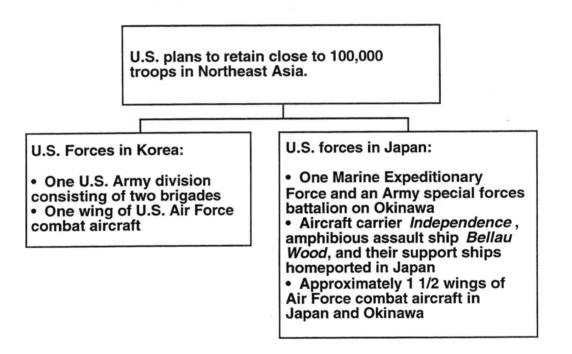

Figure A.18—Northeast Asian Presence Forces

Similarly, clicking on *Naval presence* displays Figure A.19, and then clicking on *Naval presence forces* displays Figure A.20.

The information in any of these displays can readily be changed. Linkages among the displays can be changed. Displays can be printed as vugraph transparencies or as hard copy.[3]

---

[3]The technique used here to produce these figures involved copying graphic information from MacFlow to PowerPoint slides. PowerPoint "note" format includes half-size reductions of the slide graphics; these half-size images were then copied and pasted into the Microsoft Word file that became this document.

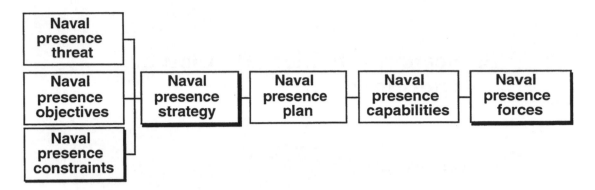

Figure A.19—Naval Presence

- **We have sought to deploy a sizable U.S. naval presence–generally, a carrier battle group accompanied by an amphibious ready group–continually in the waters off SWA, NEA, and Europe (most often, in the Med).**

- **Naval expeditionary forces can sometimes be centered around large-deck amphibious assault ships carrying AV-8B attack jets and Cobra attack helicopters, as well as a 2,000-man MEU. Another force might consist of a Tomahawk SLCM-equipped Aegis cruiser, a guided missile destroyer, attack submarines, and P-3 land-based maritime patrol aircraft.**

- **"Adaptive Joint Force Packages," tailoring joint forces to conduct overseas presence operations, could contain a mix of air, land, special operations, and maritime forces. These forces, plus designated backup units in the United States, would train jointly to provide the specific capabilities needed on-station and on-call during any particular period. Like maritime task forces, these joint force packages will also be capable of participating in combined military exercises with allied and friendly forces.**

- **Given this flexible approach, a fleet of eleven active aircraft carriers and one reserve/training carrier is sufficient.**

Figure A.20—Naval Presence Forces

B. Scenarios to Identify Analytic Questions

Korean Scenario

In the first scenario, players were given the following information:

- *North and South Korea have agreed to a peaceful reunification under terms favorable to the South but calling for withdrawal of all foreign armed forces from Korea within two years.*

- *The Secretary of Defense has directed a comprehensive review of defense strategy and policy, to include implications for acquisition.*

Each team of players was to consider itself to be a high-level planning group meeting for the first time, charged with the following:

- *Identify the most important questions raised by the situation.*

- *Identify all aspects of strategy and policy that should be reframed, reanalyzed, or reassessed.*

- *Consider all CJCS functions that must be supported, from strategic direction to reporting on roles and missions.*

Game Control provided players with an analytic representation of U.S. defense posture, based on the BUR.

Team A raised the following questions:

- Should this be viewed as a successful outcome of U.S. foreign policy?

- If this is a favorable situation, will it remain so?

- Will this change the focus of U.S. foreign policy?

- How should threat in Korea, if any, now be defined?

- Will this or should this affect the level of U.S. defense spending?

- Does this require a change to U.S. national military strategy?

- Is there any other reason or rationale to keep U.S. troops in Korea?

- Where should U.S. forces now in Korea redeploy?

- What, if anything, should the U.S. do to hedge against adverse political changes in Korea?

- To what extent does this change U.S. objectives in the Asia-Pacific region?

- If the strategy remains largely unchanged, does it need to be presented or "sold" in a different way?

- Does this change the active/reserve mix or the role of the National Guard?

These are questions that, for the most part, could—and perhaps should—be addressed, studied, or planned for in the real world, before reunification actually occurs.

Team B raised the following questions:

- At the political level, how can we "get it straight with the Hill," i.e., what does the Defense Department need to do to avoid or limit problems with Congress, especially moves to reduce the Defense budget?

- At the CINC level, what should we do with the forces now in Korea, and how do we hedge against the possibility that "it all goes bad?"

- At the level of global strategy, how will this affect the defense interests (e.g., threats, realignments, opportunities) of other states in the region?

- At the diplomatic level, how will this affect the Japanese? Will the Republic of Korea (ROK) subsume the Democratic Peoples Republic of Korea (DPRK), or will there be a new successor state? Will Korea be a nuclear power?

- Should the Chairman rearticulate U.S. military strategy in different, relevant terms?

These questions differ in kind from those raised by the first-mentioned team. They are, for the most part, political issues that probably could not be addressed very profitably in advance.

Southwest Asia Scenario

In the second scenario, players were given the following information:

- *There has been a coup in Saudi Arabia; the king and crown prince have been killed. A junta espousing limited, constitutional monarchy claims to control Riyadh, but another group claims to control the oil-rich Eastern Province, declaring itself a separate revolutionary Islamic republic.*

Again, each team of players is a high-level planning group meeting for the first time, now charged with the following:

- *Identify the most important questions raised by the situation.*
- *Identify all aspects of strategy and policy that should be reframed, reanalyzed, or reassessed.*
- *Consider all CJCS functions that must be supported, from strategic direction to reporting on roles and missions.*

The first team raised the following questions:

- Should the U.S. do nothing, wait it out?
- Should U.S.-led forces reinstate the Saudi royal family?
- Will the oil supply be disrupted? How seriously?
- Will there be civil war? If so, should the U.S. choose sides or be neutral?
- Can or should the U.S. secure the oil fields?
- How will this affect the U.S. defense budget?
- If the U.S. intervenes, will it work, and how much will it cost?
- What is the mobilization requirement? Are reserve forces needed?

The other team raised the following questions:

- Which doctrinal checklists apply?[1]
- What are our options? Can we or should we intervene? If so, with whom?
- If we act,
    - Will Germany allow staging of U.S. forces?
    - How long will this take?
    - Should we maintain a sustained force presence?
    - What are the other long-term implications?
    - What are the intertemporal issues or implications?
    - How should we isolate or contain Iraq and Iran?
    - How can we protect our ground forces?
    - How will other sheikdoms react?

The most interesting result of the game was the distinct differences in approach and decisions between the two teams, both of which were staffed by experienced

---

[1]Such checklists would allow military planners to begin developing plans while awaiting more definitive political guidance.

RAND defense analysts, some with extensive prior Joint Staff experience. One team focused on first-order strategic assumptions that might be affected by Korean reunification; the other focused on the "real" issues, including how to deal with the Chairman of the Senate Armed Services Committee.

Some, but not all, of the players used the analytic representation provided by Control to stimulate their thinking—generally either to expand upon it, to take exception to specific items (which came from the BUR), or to offer alternatives. This was Control's intent in providing the analytic representation.

C. Workshop on Overseas Presence

Initial Session

The first session was devoted to discussion of the meaning and purpose of "overseas presence."[1] The current National Security Strategy (NSS), and the NMS based on it, stress themes of peacetime engagement and enlargement (including actively promoting stability in various regions of the world), deterrence of conflicts, and fighting to win. Overseas presence, it was asserted, is crucial to all of these. The question remained: what kind and amount of presence is required for each of these objectives?

The following definition of overseas presence had been developed by the JWCA working group:

- *Proactive measures taken in the international arena to help shape the strategic environment in a manner favorable to the United States. It is the totality of U.S. instruments of power deployed overseas (both permanently or temporarily) along with the requisite infrastructure and sustainment capabilities.*

- *When linked to its purpose, overseas presence represents a strategic concept through which the nation remains engaged throughout the world to protect U.S. national interests and promote U.S. regional influence.*

- *The purposes of the military aspect of overseas presence are to:*
  - — *Reassure and support friends and allies (partnership)*
  - — *Deter would-be aggressors (prevention)*
  - — *Influence events and other states in ways favorable to the U.S. (engagement & enlargement)*
  - — *Provide an initial crisis response capability (security/warfighting).*

Many participants appeared to agree with the idea that the basis on which most current military alliances and agreements were built is a relic of the Cold War. Furthermore, the concept and purposes of U.S. overseas presence must be constructed on new premises, with consequent changes in the structure of these relationships and of U.S. force presence overseas. In addition to the new global

---

[1] This Appendix draws heavily on workshop notes prepared by Preston Niblack.

security environment, the fiscal constraints on defense spending will determine the kind and amount of overseas presence the United States can maintain.

In the absence of the global Soviet threat, some participants felt that the definition offered at the beginning of the workshop needed to add some sense of "why" the country should maintain overseas presence. One participant offered a rationale based on maintenance of international tranquillity, to facilitate international trade by safeguarding shipping and thereby stabilizing insurance rates and markets. The United States is alone in possessing the capability but lacking territorial ambitions to take the lead in forming regional partnerships to share responsibility for preserving international tranquillity.

Additionally, it is necessary to avoid creating power vacuums. The U.S. role is shifting from protector of allies against the global Soviet threat to a more regional focus. Now it serves as balancer and catalyst, to promote renewal of regional security alliances and coalitions.

As is well known, U.S. interests center in North America (where there is scarcely a military threat), Europe, East Asia, and the Persian Gulf. Some questioned whether objectives to protect U.S. interests would "play in Peoria" sufficiently to fund an adequate presence.

There is little consensus on what constitutes an adequate or sufficient presence. Presumably there is a level of presence below which it would be insufficient to promote our influence and regional political-military goals, deter conflict, or provide adequate in-place crisis response capability—but that level or those levels are not well understood. In-place forces enhance the sense of our stake (which is good if it prompts successful operations but bad if it drags us into losing situations), provide the basis for combined planning and training and interoperability, and are the core for reinforcement. Too low a level of presence reduces influence and willingness of others to follow our leadership.

Rotational forces can fill out permanently stationed forces as needed. Are CONUS-based power projection forces adequate substitutes for permanent or rotational presence? Some operational tasks may require actual presence. In addition, it was pointed out, the withdrawal of in-place forces has implications for the CONUS-based force structure—they must be lighter (more transportable), with more emphasis on air and naval forces. Such changes in force structure may narrow the available military options.

One suggestion was to leave support forces in place and withdraw combat forces, but others argued that there was little or no deterrent value to support forces, even if their presence might facilitate possible rapid introduction of combat forces.

Wrapping up, the group felt that in addition to the "what" provided by the initial definition, some sense of "why" overseas presence was important to U.S. interests was needed, focusing on the role of presence in renewing U.S. security partnerships for dealing with the dangers of the new global security environment (as well as protecting the U.S. ability to act unilaterally on behalf of its interests). There were several additional purposes of presence that participants felt needed to be captured in the definition: alliance management, facilitating access, and catalyzing cooperation among regional actors.

To help define the objectives of overseas presence more concretely, workshop participants were formed into four teams to play in two game scenarios.

The format for each game was as follows:

- *For each of two one-move games*
  - *Each team plays the United States*
  - *Team leaders (1) facilitate discussion and (2) summarize deliberations*
  - *Teams meet for one hour*
- *45 minutes to deliberate*
- *15 minutes to pull together and move paper*
- *Plenary session for 30 minutes*
- *Each team leader gives 10-minute summary of major issues, their importance, and views/recommendations*
- *Information provided to teams*
  - *Summary of present, real-world overseas presence in region*
  - *Control-originated statement of present trends in region, which may differ from Defense Planning Guidance (DPG) assumptions, National Intelligence Estimates (NIEs), etc.*
- *Control reps may present additional questions for teams to consider.*

Southwest Asia Scenario

The first scenario posited the following trends, which players were asked to accept as true for game purposes:

- *Iran and Iraq are preparing for expected offensive or defensive war with one another and for possible war with the U.S. and allies.*

> — Both countries have studied the Iran-Iraq war and Operation Desert Storm (ODS) extensively and are doing their utmost to avoid earlier mistakes.
> — Preparations include elaborate cover/deception (as defense against U.S. stealth and precision munitions) and diverse means to inflict casualties on U.S. personnel (as an end in itself).

- *Saudi policy of steering a middle-conservative but repressive course between the demands of radical Muslim fundamentalists and relatively progressive secular constitutional monarchists will eventually fail.*
  - *Failure may be peaceful or violent (e.g., by coup, civil war, and/or invasion).*
  - *Factions will receive military, political, and/or economic support from various foreign interests.*

Two of the biggest issues raised by players in the Southwest Asian scenario were (1) whether continuous Carrier Battle Group (CVBG) presence in the Gulf was necessary or desirable and (2) whether increased interoperability could be achieved with Gulf Cooperation Council (GCC) states through increased joint exercises, training, security assistance, etc. Players discussed what enhancements to a "standard" CVBG might be desirable and whether enough mine countermeasures ships were available for all contingencies.

There seemed to be agreement that it would be reasonable to draw down presence in the Mediterranean to augment that in the Gulf.

Another issue discussed was whether to (a) assume access to Saudi Arabia, (b) spend more now to have a forcible entry capability, or (c) develop other bases in the region. There was discussion of the difficulty of fighting without some access to Saudi Arabia. It was also noted that if protecting the eastern oil fields is the goal, then eventually one would have to fight one's way in. However, it was thought that the United States cannot assume the kind of buildup period it had in ODS. Alternatives are (a) speed up deployment by lift or prepositioning, (b) rely more on airpower, say, through a greater carrier (CV) OPTEMPO, or (c) expand access to other Gulf states through military-to-military contacts, security assistance, exercises, and training.

Northeast Asia Scenario

The second scenario posited the following trends, which players were asked to accept as true for game purposes:

- *Tensions between North and South Korea will subside, with eventual Korean reunification and reduction or elimination of the U.S. force presence in Korea, as presently justified and configured.*

- *Japan and Russia will reach a settlement of the Kurile Islands dispute, paving the way for extensive cooperation in developing and exploiting the resources of Asian Russia, to the advantage of Japan and European Russia.*

- *U.S. efforts to increase burdensharing by Japan will succeed, such that Japanese military capability will increase and Japanese security dependence on the U.S. will decrease.*
  - *Japan will decrease its host nation support of U.S. forces and will eventually request reductions in presence in-country.*
  - *The price for continued presence will be acceptance of continued large trade imbalances.*

- *Chinese assimilation of Hong Kong will serve as a model or laboratory for its eventual intended assimilation of Taiwan.*

In playing the East Asian scenario, players identified the following objectives:

- Maintain U.S. access and influence in Northeast Asia
- Ensure regional stability in the Pacific Rim
- Prevent development of Japanese power projection capability through Theater Missile Defense (TMD), intelligence sharing, and maintaining base access
- Prevent proliferation of weapons of mass destruction
- Increase confidence-building efforts with China

All felt that a rearmed Japan would be destabilizing in the region. Continued U.S. presence would help reassure Japan as well as other major regional actors; therefore, the United States should not and could not completely withdraw from the region. The United States should consider other ways to maintain access, either through seeking new base access (e.g., Cam Ranh Bay or Vladivostok) or regular rotations and exercises. Many players speculated, however, that ultimately there would be no permanently stationed forces west of Hawaii (or Guam). No one mentioned Russia as a possible regional military power.

Participants believed it important to get people from different countries to work together in multilateral exercises. In such exercises the United States acts as the catalyst and common ally—the only disinterested party in the region, playing a role of common security guarantor. Participants also suggested that military-to-military contacts be increased.

Again, force structure issues rose to the fore, with a smaller ground force presence than currently and more emphasis on air, naval, and expeditionary forces. Also, intelligence and reconnaissance capabilities would become relatively more important as forces are drawn down, as would creating arrangements to ensure these capabilities. Again, lift assumes increasing urgency.

POM issues included the following:

- Transfer force structure from the Western Pacific, including the 8th Army

- Prepositioning ashore and afloat for contingencies

- Exercise rotational forces within the Pacific Rim and Russia, maintaining ground forces training capability in theater

- Program sharing of forces with U.S. Central Command (USCENTCOM)

- Establish TMD and intelligence-sharing arrangements with Japan.

CINC-Teams Session

In a subsequent workshop session, each group represented a CINC and was asked to apply the following JWCA assessment group methodology:

1. Determine requirements/opportunities
   - Treaties and security agreements
   - Current positions and policies
   - National interests and goals
   - Political and economic goals

2. Determine military objectives

3. Determine military capabilities to meet objectives

4. Assess current capabilities and determine risks

5. Recommend changes (divest or recapitalize)
   - CPA
   - POM 96
   - Long-term acquisition programs

The USCENTCOM group produced the following:
- Military objectives
  — Protect shipping
  — Ensure chokepoints and lines of communication (LOCs) remain open

— Provide rapid crisis response deployment capability, elements to include lift, prepositioning, access, and interoperability

- Military capabilities
  — Improve interoperability with regional allies
  — Provide ballistic missile defense (BMD) capability to regional allies
  — Promote multilateral military-to-military contacts
  — Improve tactical intelligence capabilities
  — Sustain visible U.S. military presence
  — Maintain capability to conduct noncombatant evacuation operations (NEO)
  — Defeat resurgent Iran or Iraq
  — Maintain/increase defense and access agreements
  — Conduct exercises
  — Provide adequate prepositioning to support rapid defense of GCC states

- POM issues/risks
  — Is interoperability with regional allies adequate?
  — Is mine countermeasures (MCM) capability adequate?
  — Is prepositioning adequate and of the right type and mix?
  — Is BMD capability adequate? Can it arrive in time?

The U.S. Atlantic Command (USACOM) group produced the following:

- Military objectives
  — Provide prepared/trained forces for supported CINCs for both scheduled and unscheduled commitments
  — Support multilateral peace and humanitarian operations, given issues of force commitment versus OPTEMPO and PERSTEMPO
  — Maintain focus on and ability to respond to contingencies within and external to USACOM's area of responsibility (AOR)

- Military capabilities
  — Capabilities are stretched thin
    • Increase forces
    • Decrease training requirements
    • Consider financing training by closing facilities
  — What are characteristics of forces required, such as continental versus maritime?
  — Balance of long-term commitments: Guantanamo, Lajes, Iceland
  — Capabilities
    • Sufficient for standard operations and training requirements

- Overseas basing sufficient; issue of whether Guantanamo and Lajes are necessary
- Command, Control, Communications, Computer Systems, and Intelligence (C4I) improvements warranted for joint/combined interoperability
- Reserve Component (RC), civil affairs, psyops availability not assured
  — Requirements
    - Scheduled: training deployment
    - Unscheduled: Haiti, drug interdiction
    - Maintenance: equipment (ship) maintenance deferral due to commitments
  — Risks: unscheduled commitments have reduced deterrence, preparedness for MRC as forces are pressed to respond to them

- POM issues/risks
  — Joint Training and Simulation Center (JTASC) support essential
  — Increasing demands of unscheduled commitments affect readiness
  — Recapitalization focused on two MRCs threat but usage is based on a multitude of lesser contingencies, which are not necessarily lesser included cases of the MRC requirements and capabilities
  — Reduce fixed base costs to fund rotational forces (primarily naval and amphibious)
  — C4I joint/combined training opportunities vs. force structure training
  — Examine balance of continental vs. mobile forces

- Invest in exploitation of information technologies to improve force operability.

The U.S. Pacific Command (USPACOM) group produced the following:
- Military objectives and POM issues
  — Deter/address Korean threat
    - Antitactical Ballistic Missiles (ATBMs)
    - Early warning
    - Base and port defense
      — Navy funding for Aegis Block 4A
      — Patriot deployments
    - Strategic mobility (airlift and sealift)
    - Force levels
      — Reductions in USAF FWE, C-130s at Yokota
      — Marine Expeditionary Unit (MEU) to be kept in Japan

- Chemical Warfare/Biological Warfare (CW/BW) defense and detection
- Protective clothing
- ROK improvements
- Prepositioning
- Mine countermeasures

— Regional stability: Presence in Japan

— Addressing regional threats, instabilities, ensuring access, deterring regional conflict, maintaining sea lines of communication (SLOCs), reassuring allies and friends of safe regional security environment

- Air Force restructuring
- Rotations to Alaska
- USMC artillery reductions; possible move from Okinawa
- Maintain 7th Fleet
- CVN, CVBG presence, OPTEMPO
- Regional access and prepositioning (Thailand)
- Long-term balance of CONUS vs. overseas USAF assets
- Long-term Weapons of Mass Destruction (WMD) problems

— Regional stability: Military-to-military relations

— Deterring low-priority difficulties; enhancing wider regional security

- Security assistance funding
- Title 10 issues; disaster relief; Crisis Action Teams (CATs)

The U.S. Southern Command (USSOUTHCOM) group considered relocating headquarters back to CONUS faster and disestablishing Joint Task Force (JTF) Bravo.

The U.S. European Command (USEUCOM group) produced the following POM issues:

- More investment in Partners for Peace (PFP), military-to-military, and Special Operations Force (SOF)

- Less investment in base infrastructure

- No change in
  - NATO infrastructure and forces
  - Brigade size and multinational corps training
  - Continued need for corps deployed forward for credibility
  - USEUCOM crucial for NATO training